EFFECTIVE MANAGEMENT OF EPILEPSY IN ADULT AND CHILDREN

A Multifaceted Approach to Seizure Control, Medication Management, Lifestyle Modifications, and Supportive Care for all ages

By

Sherrie A Jones.

ABOUT THE BOOK

Epilepsy is a neurological disorder characterized by recurrent, unprovoked seizures. It affects people of all ages, races, and ethnic backgrounds, making it one of the most common neurological disorders globally. Epilepsy can have a profound impact on an individual's quality of life, affecting their ability to work, drive, and engage in daily activities. However, with proper management, many people with epilepsy can lead full, active lives.

This guide aims to provide comprehensive information about epilepsy, including its causes, symptoms, diagnosis, treatment options, and practical tips for living with the condition. It will also discuss the various types of seizures and their management, as well as address common misconceptions and stigmas surrounding epilepsy.

Understanding epilepsy is essential for individuals with the condition, their families, caregivers, and the community at large. By increasing awareness and knowledge about epilepsy, we can help reduce stigma, improve access to care, and enhance the quality of life for those living with this disorder.

Whether you are newly diagnosed with epilepsy, a caregiver, or simply seeking more information about the condition, this guide is designed to be a valuable resource. By working together, we can support those affected by epilepsy and empower them to live their lives to the fullest.

TABLE OF CONTENT

Chapter 1

Introduction to Epilepsy

1.1 Definition

The definition of epilepsy is a neurological disorder characterized by recurrent, unprovoked seizures. Seizures are caused by sudden, excessive electrical discharges in the brain that disrupt normal brain functions. These discharges can result in a wide range of symptoms, including loss of consciousness, convulsions, and abnormal sensations or movements.

Key points in the definition of epilepsy include:

1. **Recurrent seizures:** Epilepsy is diagnosed when a person experiences two or more unprovoked seizures more than 24 hours apart. Unprovoked means that the seizure was not triggered by a reversible cause such as fever, low blood sugar, or alcohol withdrawal.

2. **Unprovoked seizures:** Seizures that occur without an identifiable trigger are considered unprovoked. This is in contrast to provoked seizures, which are triggered by factors such as fever, head injury, or drug withdrawal.

3. **Neurological disorder:** Epilepsy is considered a neurological disorder because it affects the nervous system, particularly the brain. The abnormal electrical activity in the brain during seizures can lead to a wide range of symptoms and behaviors.

4. **Variability in symptoms:** The symptoms of epilepsy can vary widely from person to person and may include convulsions, staring spells, temporary confusion, and sensory disturbances. The type and severity of seizures can also vary, ranging from brief lapses of attention to full-body convulsions.

5. **Chronic condition:** Epilepsy is typically a chronic condition, meaning that it is ongoing and requires long-term

management. However, some people may outgrow epilepsy, particularly if it begins in childhood.

6. **Diagnosis:** The diagnosis of epilepsy is based on a careful medical history, physical examination, and diagnostic tests such as EEG (electroencephalogram) and imaging studies (MRI or CT scan) to rule out other causes of seizures.

7. **Treatment:** While epilepsy cannot be cured, it can often be managed effectively with medication, surgery, or other treatments. The goal of treatment is to reduce the frequency and severity of seizures while minimizing side effects and improving quality of life.

Overall, epilepsy is a complex neurological disorder that can have a significant impact on a person's life. However, with proper diagnosis and treatment, many people with epilepsy are able to lead full, active lives.

1.2 Types of Seizures

Seizures are classified into several types based on their characteristics and the areas of the brain affected. The two main categories are focal seizures (previously called partial seizures) and generalized seizures. Each type of seizure has its own distinct features and symptoms.

1. **Focal Seizures (Partial Seizures):**
   - **Simple Focal Seizures:** These seizures do not cause a loss of consciousness. The person may experience altered emotions or perceptions, twitching or jerking of a body part, or sensory changes such as tingling or flashing lights.
   - **Complex Focal Seizures:** These seizures typically involve a change in consciousness or awareness. The person may exhibit repetitive movements, such as lip smacking or hand rubbing, or engage in unusual behaviors like wandering aimlessly.

2. **Generalized Seizures:**
   - **Absence Seizures:** Also known as petit mal seizures, absence seizures primarily affect children. They are characterized by a brief loss of consciousness and staring spells. The person may appear to be daydreaming and is usually unaware of their surroundings.
   - **Tonic Seizures:** Tonic seizures cause stiffening of muscles, usually in the back, arms, and legs. The person may fall if standing when the seizure occurs.
   - **Clonic Seizures:** Clonic seizures are characterized by repeated, rhythmic jerking movements of the arms and legs.
   - **Myoclonic Seizures:** Myoclonic seizures involve sudden, brief jerks or twitches of a muscle or muscle group. These seizures can affect the arms, legs, or upper body.

- **Tonic-Clonic Seizures:** Formerly known as grand mal seizures, tonic-clonic seizures are the most widely recognized type. They involve a combination of muscle stiffening (tonic phase) followed by rhythmic, jerking movements (clonic phase). Loss of consciousness often occurs, along with other symptoms such as tongue biting, loss of bladder or bowel control, and confusion after the seizure.

3. **Other Seizure Types:**
   - **Atonic Seizures:** Atonic seizures, also called drop attacks, cause a sudden loss of muscle tone, leading to a person collapsing or falling down.
   - **Epileptic Spasms:** These seizures are characterized by brief, repetitive muscle contractions that can cause a person's body to bend or flex.

It's important to note that seizure symptoms can vary widely among individuals, and a person may experience different types of seizures over time. Proper diagnosis by a healthcare professional is essential for determining the most appropriate treatment and management strategies for each inindividual.

1.3 Prevalence

The prevalence of epilepsy, or the number of people living with epilepsy at a given time, can vary depending on factors such as age, geographic region, and underlying causes. Here's a detailed explanation of epilepsy prevalence:

1. **Global Prevalence:** Epilepsy is one of the most common neurological disorders globally, affecting people of all ages. According to the World Health Organization (WHO), around 50 million people worldwide have epilepsy.
2. **Age-specific Prevalence:** Epilepsy can occur at any age, but its prevalence varies among different age groups:

- In children: Epilepsy is more common in children than in adults. The prevalence is highest in the first year of life and declines gradually thereafter.
  - In adults: The prevalence of epilepsy tends to increase with age, peaking in older adults.

3. **Regional Variations:** The prevalence of epilepsy varies widely between regions and countries. Factors such as access to healthcare, socioeconomic conditions, and the prevalence of risk factors for epilepsy (such as head injuries or infections) can influence regional differences.

4. **High-Income Countries vs. Low- and Middle-Income Countries:** The prevalence of epilepsy is generally higher in low- and middle-income countries compared to high-income countries. This difference may be due to factors such as limited access to healthcare, higher rates of certain risk factors (such as infections

or perinatal injuries), and variations in diagnostic practices and reporting.

5. **Impact of Risk Factors:** Certain risk factors can increase the likelihood of developing epilepsy, which can vary depending on the population:
   - In high-income countries, factors such as traumatic brain injury, stroke, and brain tumors are more common risk factors for epilepsy.
   - In low- and middle-income countries, factors such as infections (such as neurocysticercosis), perinatal injuries, and lack of access to healthcare can contribute to a higher prevalence of epilepsy.

6. **Impact on Quality of Life:** Epilepsy can have a significant impact on quality of life, affecting various aspects such as physical health, mental health, social relationships, and employment opportunities. Stigma and discrimination related to epilepsy can also contribute to the overall burden of the condition.

7. **Challenges in Diagnosis and Treatment:**
Despite its prevalence, epilepsy is often underdiagnosed and undertreated, particularly in low- and middle-income countries. Improving access to healthcare, increasing awareness about epilepsy, and addressing stigma are crucial steps in improving the lives of people living with epilepsy worldwide.

Epilepsy is a common neurological disorder that can have a significant impact on individuals, families, and communities. Understanding its prevalence and associated factors is essential for developing effective strategies for diagnosis, treatment, and support for people living with epilepsy.

Chapter 2

Causes and Risk Factors

2.1 Genetic Factors

Genetic factors play a significant role in the development of epilepsy. Here's a detailed explanation of how genetic factors can contribute to epilepsy:

1. **Genetic Influences:** Epilepsy can be caused by genetic factors, with certain genetic mutations or variations increasing the risk of developing the condition. These genetic influences can be inherited from one or both parents or can occur spontaneously (de novo mutations).

2. **Complex Genetic Patterns:** The genetics of epilepsy can be complex, involving interactions between multiple genes and environmental factors. Some forms of epilepsy are caused by mutations in a single gene (monogenic epilepsy), while

others are thought to involve multiple genes (polygenic epilepsy).

3. **Genetic Syndromes:** Some genetic syndromes are associated with a high risk of epilepsy. For example, Dravet syndrome, a severe form of epilepsy that begins in infancy, is often caused by mutations in the SCN1A gene. Other syndromes, such as tuberous sclerosis complex and neurofibromatosis type 1, are also associated with an increased risk of epilepsy.

4. **Family History:** A family history of epilepsy is a significant risk factor for developing the condition. Individuals with a first-degree relative (parent, sibling, or child) with epilepsy are at a higher risk compared to the general population.

5. **Genetic Testing:** Advances in genetic testing have made it possible to identify specific genetic mutations associated with epilepsy. Genetic testing can help in diagnosing certain types of epilepsy,

predicting the course of the condition, and guiding treatment decisions.

6. **Pharmacogenetics:** Genetic factors can also influence how individuals respond to antiepileptic drugs (AEDs). Certain genetic variations can affect the metabolism and effectiveness of AEDs, leading to differences in treatment outcomes.

7. **Gene-Environment Interactions:** While genetic factors play a significant role in epilepsy, environmental factors can also contribute to the development of the condition. Factors such as head injuries, infections, and prenatal exposure to toxins can interact with genetic predispositions to increase the risk of epilepsy.

8. **Genetic Counseling:** For individuals with epilepsy or a family history of epilepsy, genetic counseling can be beneficial. Genetic counselors can help individuals understand the genetic basis of their condition, assess the risk of recurrence in

future generations, and make informed decisions about family planning.

Genetic factors play a complex role in the development of epilepsy, with a wide range of genetic mutations and variations contributing to the condition. Understanding these genetic factors is essential for improving diagnosis, treatment, and management of epepilepsy.

2.2 Brain injuries and infections

1. **Traumatic Brain Injury (TBI):** This results from a sudden, violent blow or jolt to the head or body. It can lead to temporary or permanent brain dysfunction. Symptoms can range from mild (e.g., brief changes in mental status or consciousness) to severe (e.g., prolonged unconsciousness or amnesia).
2. **Concussion:** A type of mild TBI caused by a bump, blow, or jolt to the head. It can disrupt normal brain function, leading to

symptoms such as headache, confusion, memory problems, and nausea.

3. **Acquired Brain Injury (ABI):** Refers to any brain damage that occurs after birth and is not related to a congenital disorder or degenerative disease. It can result from non-traumatic causes such as stroke, infection, or lack of oxygen.

Types of Brain Infections:

1. **Meningitis:** Inflammation of the meninges, the protective membranes covering the brain and spinal cord. It can be caused by viruses, bacteria, fungi, or parasites. Symptoms include fever, headache, stiff neck, and sensitivity to light.

2. **Encephalitis:** Inflammation of the brain tissue, often caused by a viral infection. It can result in flu-like symptoms, confusion, seizures, or even coma in severe cases.

3. **Brain Abscess:** A collection of pus within the brain tissue, usually caused by a

bacterial or fungal infection. Symptoms
include headache, fever, nausea, and
neurological deficits depending on the
location of the abscess.

4. **Neurocysticercosis:** An infection of the
brain caused by the larval stage of the
pork tapeworm. It can lead to seizures,
headaches, and other neurological
symptoms.

Treatment:

- **Brain Injuries:** Treatment depends on the
type and severity of the injury. It may
include rest, medication for symptoms
(e.g., pain relievers, anti-seizure drugs),
physical therapy, and in severe cases,
surgery to repair damaged tissue or relieve
pressure on the brain.

- **Brain Infections:** Treatment typically
involves medications such as antibiotics
(for bacterial infections), antivirals (for
viral infections), or antifungals (for fungal
infections). In some cases, surgery may be

necessary to drain abscesses or remove infected tissue.

Both brain injuries and infections can have long-term consequences, including cognitive deficits, motor impairments, and psychological changes. Rehabilitation and ongoing medical care are often necessary to manage these conditions and improve outcomes.

2.3 Developmental disorders

Developmental disorders are a group of conditions characterized by delays or differences in the development of physical, cognitive, language, and social skills. These disorders typically begin in infancy or childhood and can significantly impact an individual's daily functioning and quality of life. Developmental disorders are usually diagnosed in early childhood, but they can persist into adolescence and adulthood.

There are several types of developmental disorders, including:

1. **Autism Spectrum Disorder (ASD)**: ASD is a complex neurodevelopmental disorder that affects social interaction, communication, and behavior. Individuals with ASD may have difficulty with social interactions, exhibit repetitive behaviors, and have limited interests or activities. The severity of symptoms can vary widely among individuals.

2. **Attention-Deficit/Hyperactivity Disorder (ADHD)**: ADHD is a common neurodevelopmental disorder characterized by persistent patterns of inattention, hyperactivity, and impulsivity that can interfere with functioning or development. It often presents in early childhood and can continue into adulthood.

3. **Intellectual Disability (ID)**: ID is a condition characterized by limitations in intellectual functioning (such as reasoning, learning, and problem-solving) and adaptive behavior (skills necessary for independent daily living). The severity of

ID can vary widely, from mild to profound.

4. **Communication Disorders**: These disorders affect the ability to use and understand language. They include conditions such as speech sound disorder, language disorder, and social (pragmatic) communication disorder.

5. **Motor Disorders**: Motor disorders affect movement and coordination. Examples include developmental coordination disorder (DCD) and stereotypic movement disorder.

6. **Specific Learning Disorders**: These disorders affect the acquisition and use of academic skills, such as reading, writing, or mathematics. Dyslexia (reading disorder) and dyscalculia (mathematics disorder) are examples of specific learning disorders.

7. **Other Developmental Disorders**: This category includes a range of conditions that do not fit into the above categories but still involve delays or differences in

development. Examples include Rett syndrome and selective mutism.

The exact causes of developmental disorders are often complex and can involve a combination of genetic, environmental, and neurological factors. Early detection and intervention are crucial for managing developmental disorders and improving outcomes. Treatment approaches may include behavioral therapies, educational interventions, and, in some cases, medication. It's important for individuals with developmental disorders to receive comprehensive and individualized care from a team of healthcare prprofessionals.

2.4 Other potential causes

1. **Brain Tumors**: Tumors in the brain can disrupt normal brain activity and lead to seizures. The risk of seizures depends on the size, location, and type of tumor.
2. **Stroke**: A stroke occurs when there is a disruption in blood flow to the brain, leading to brain damage. Seizures can

occur as a result of the brain injury caused by a stroke.

3. **Traumatic Brain Injury (TBI)**: Head injuries, such as those sustained in car accidents or falls, can lead to epilepsy, especially if there is damage to the brain.

4. **Infections**: Certain infections that affect the brain, such as meningitis, encephalitis, and brain abscesses, can trigger epilepsy.

5. **Developmental Disorders**: Some developmental disorders, such as neurofibromatosis or tuberous sclerosis, can be associated with epilepsy.

6. **Genetic Factors**: Some forms of epilepsy have a genetic component, meaning they can run in families.

7. **Perinatal Injury**: Brain injury that occurs around the time of birth, such as hypoxic-ischemic encephalopathy (lack of oxygen to the brain), can increase the risk of epilepsy later in life.

8. **Metabolic Disorders**: Certain metabolic disorders, such as phenylketonuria (PKU)

or mitochondrial disorders, can lead to epilepsy.

9. **Autoimmune Disorders**: Autoimmune disorders that affect the brain, such as autoimmune encephalitis, can trigger seizures.

10. **Toxicity**: Exposure to certain toxins, such as lead or carbon monoxide, can increase the risk of epilepsy.

11. **Alzheimer's Disease and Dementia:** These conditions can sometimes be associated with seizures, especially in later stages of the disease.

Chapter 3

Types of Epilepsy

3.1 Generalized seizures

Generalized seizures are seizures that involve widespread electrical activity in the brain, affecting both sides of the brain from the onset of the seizure. These seizures can cause loss of consciousness and typically affect the entire body. There are several types of generalized seizures:

1. **Tonic-Clonic Seizures (formerly known as Grand Mal Seizures)**: Tonic-clonic seizures are the most well-known type of generalized seizure. They are characterized by two distinct phases:
   - Tonic Phase: The muscles suddenly contract, causing the person to lose consciousness and fall if standing. Breathing may temporarily stop, and the person may make a

grunting sound. This phase usually lasts for about 10-20 seconds.

- o Clonic Phase: The muscles begin to jerk and spasm rhythmically. This phase can last for a few seconds to several minutes. Afterward, the person may be confused, fatigued, or experience muscle soreness.

2. **Absence Seizures (formerly known as Petit Mal Seizures):** Absence seizures are characterized by a brief loss of consciousness and awareness. The person may appear to stare blankly for a few seconds, with or without subtle movements such as eye blinking or lip smacking. Afterward, the person usually resumes normal activity without any memory of the episode.

3. **Myoclonic Seizures**: Myoclonic seizures involve sudden, brief muscle jerks or twitches that can affect a specific part of the body or the entire body. These seizures may occur in clusters and can be mistaken for simple motor tics.

4. **Atonic Seizures** (also known as Drop Attacks): Atonic seizures involve a sudden loss of muscle tone, causing the person to collapse or fall. These seizures are characterized by a brief period of limpness and can lead to injuries if the person falls.
5. **Tonic Seizures:** Tonic seizures are characterized by sudden stiffening of the muscles. These seizures typically last less than 20 seconds and may cause the person to fall if standing.
6. **Clonic Seizures:** Clonic seizures involve rhythmic, jerking muscle movements. These seizures are rare and can affect specific muscle groups or the entire body.

3.2 Focal seizures

Focal seizures, also known as partial seizures, originate in a specific area of the brain and can affect one part or one side of the body. These seizures are caused by abnormal electrical activity in the brain and can be classified into two main types:

1. **Focal Onset Aware Seizures (Simple Partial Seizures)**: In these seizures, the person remains conscious and aware during the seizure. Symptoms can vary depending on which part of the brain is affected, but may include:
   - Muscle contractions or jerking
   - Sensory changes, such as tingling, numbness, or a sensation of déjà vu
   - Emotional changes, such as fear, anxiety, or déjà vu
   - Autonomic symptoms, such as changes in heart rate or stomach sensations
2. **Focal Onset Impaired Awareness Seizures (Complex Partial Seizures)**: These seizures involve altered consciousness or awareness. The person may appear confused, dazed, or unresponsive. Symptoms can include:
   - Staring blankly

- o Lip smacking, chewing, or swallowing movements
- o Fumbling with objects
- o Incoherent speech or mumbling
- o Automatic movements, such as walking in circles or wandering

Focal seizures can spread to other areas of the brain and become generalized seizures, affecting the entire brain. This progression can lead to a loss of consciousness and convulsions, resembling tonic-clonic seizures.

Causes of focal seizures can include brain tumors, brain injuries, stroke, infections, and genetic factors. Diagnosis is typically made through a combination of medical history, physical examination, EEG (electroencephalogram), and imaging tests such as MRI (magnetic resonance imaging).

Treatment for focal seizures often involves antiepileptic medications to help control seizures. In some cases, surgery may be recommended to remove the area of the brain responsible for the seizures, if it can be safely done without causing significant neurological deficits.

Managing focal seizures may also involve identifying and avoiding triggers, such as lack of sleep, stress, or certain medications. It's important for individuals with focal seizures to work closely with healthcare professionals to develop a comprehensive treatment plan tailored to their specific needs.

3.3 Unknown onset seizures

Unknown onset seizures, also known as unclassified seizures, are seizures for which the exact onset is not clearly understood or identified. These seizures can present challenges in diagnosis and treatment because there is uncertainty about the underlying cause or origin of the seizure activity.

Some key points about unknown onset seizures include:

1. **Presentation**: The seizure may manifest as a sudden and unexplained change in behavior, consciousness, or motor activity. The person may experience convulsions, muscle spasms, or altered sensations without a clear trigger or warning.

2. **Diagnosis:** Diagnosing unknown onset seizures often involves a thorough medical history, physical examination, and neurological tests such as EEG (electroencephalogram) and imaging studies like MRI (magnetic resonance imaging). These tests can help identify abnormalities in brain activity or structure that may be associated with seizures.

3. **Causes**: Unknown onset seizures can have various underlying causes, including genetic factors, brain abnormalities, infections, or metabolic disorders. In some cases, the cause may not be identified despite thorough evaluation.

4. **Classification**: Without a clear understanding of the seizure onset, it may be challenging to classify the seizure type

(e.g., generalized or focal). In such cases, the focus is often on managing the seizures and addressing any underlying conditions.

5. **Treatment**: Treatment for unknown onset seizures typically involves antiepileptic medications to help control seizure activity. The choice of medication and treatment approach may vary depending on the individual's specific circumstances and response to treatment.

6. **Monitoring and Management**: Regular monitoring and follow-up with healthcare providers are essential to track seizure activity, adjust treatment as needed, and address any related issues or concerns. Lifestyle modifications, such as getting enough sleep, managing stress, and avoiding potential triggers, may also be recommended.

7. **Prognosis**: The outlook for individuals with unknown onset seizures can vary depending on the underlying cause, response to treatment, and overall health.

With appropriate management, many people with seizures can achieve good seizure control and lead fulfilling lives.

It's important for individuals with unknown onset seizures to work closely with healthcare providers to establish an accurate diagnosis, develop a comprehensive treatment plan, and receive ongoing support and care.

3.4 Special syndromes

Special syndromes in epilepsy refer to specific patterns of seizures and associated features that occur in certain age groups or have distinctive clinical characteristics. These syndromes are classified based on factors such as seizure types, EEG findings, age of onset, and associated symptoms. Some examples of special syndromes in epilepsy include:

1. **Benign Rolandic Epilepsy (BRE)**: Also known as benign epilepsy with centrotemporal spikes (BECTS), BRE typically occurs in children between the

ages of 3 and 13 years. Seizures often involve twitching or numbness on one side of the face or in one hand, and they usually occur at night. BRE is often outgrown by adolescence and does not typically cause long-term problems.

2. **Childhood Absence Epilepsy (CAE):** CAE is characterized by frequent absence seizures, which are brief episodes of staring or altered consciousness. These seizures usually begin between the ages of 4 and 10 years and may be associated with subtle movements such as eye blinking or lip smacking. CAE often responds well to medication, and many children outgrow the condition by adolescence.

3. **Lennox-Gastaut Syndrome (LGS):** LGS is a severe form of epilepsy that usually begins in early childhood, typically between the ages of 1 and 8 years. It is characterized by multiple seizure types, including tonic seizures (muscle stiffness), atonic seizures (sudden loss of muscle tone), and atypical absence seizures. LGS

is often difficult to treat and can be associated with intellectual disability and developmental delays.

4. **Dravet Syndrome**: Dravet syndrome is a rare and severe form of epilepsy that begins in infancy, usually within the first year of life. It is characterized by prolonged seizures, often triggered by fever or illness, as well as developmental delays and behavioral problems. Dravet syndrome is typically caused by a genetic mutation and can be challenging to manage.

5. **Juvenile Myoclonic Epilepsy (JME)**: JME typically begins in adolescence or young adulthood and is characterized by myoclonic jerks (sudden, brief muscle jerks), often upon awakening. Seizures may also include generalized tonic-clonic seizures and, less commonly, absence seizures. JME usually requires lifelong treatment with antiepileptic medications.

6. **Landau-Kleffner Syndrome (LKS)**: LKS is a rare childhood neurological

disorder characterized by the gradual or sudden development of language problems and behavioral disturbances. Seizures, including focal seizures and atypical absence seizures, may also occur. LKS is often associated with abnormal EEG findings and can lead to significant language and cognitive deficits.

7. **Epilepsy with Myoclonic-Absences**: This syndrome is characterized by a combination of myoclonic jerks and absence seizures. It typically begins in childhood and may be associated with cognitive impairment. Treatment with antiepileptic medications is usually necessary.

8. **Temporal Lobe Epilepsy (TLE)**: TLE is a type of focal epilepsy that originates in the temporal lobes of the brain. It is characterized by complex partial seizures, which can involve altered consciousness, repetitive movements, and unusual behaviors. TLE can be associated with a variety of symptoms, including memory

difficulties, déjà vu experiences, and emotional disturbances.

These are just a few examples of special syndromes in epilepsy. Each syndrome has its own unique characteristics, age of onset, and prognosis. Proper diagnosis and management of these syndromes are essential for optimizing treatment outcomes and improving quality of life for individuals with epilepsy.

Chapter 4

Diagnosis of Epilepsy

4.1 Medical history and physical examination

1.Medical History:

- **Seizure Description**: Details about the seizure(s), including the type, frequency, duration, and any triggers or warning signs.
- **Medical Conditions:** Any preexisting medical conditions, such as brain injuries, infections, or genetic disorders, which may be associated with seizures.
- **Medications**: A list of current medications, including prescription, over-the-counter, and herbal supplements, as some medications can lower seizure threshold or interact with antiepileptic drugs.

- **Family History:** Information about family members with epilepsy or other neurological conditions, as there may be a genetic predisposition.
- **Developmental History**: Details about developmental milestones, as developmental delays or disorders may be associated with certain types of epilepsy.
- **Lifestyle Factors:** Information about sleep patterns, stress levels, alcohol or drug use, and other factors that may influence seizure activity.
- **Previous Test Results:** Any previous EEG, MRI, or other diagnostic test results related to seizures or neurological conditions.
- **Seizure Impact:** The impact of seizures on daily life, including any limitations or safety concerns.
- **Psychosocial History:** Information about mental health, social support,

and coping mechanisms, as these factors can affect seizure management.

2.Physical Examination:

- **Neurological Examination**: Evaluation of neurological function, including assessment of motor skills, reflexes, sensation, coordination, and mental status.
- **Vital Signs:** Measurement of blood pressure, heart rate, temperature, and respiratory rate to assess overall health and identify any abnormalities.
- **General Physical Examination:** Examination of other body systems to check for signs of underlying conditions that may be related to seizures.
- **Skin Examination**: Examination for any physical signs of trauma or injury that may be related to seizures.

- ○ **Growth and Development:**
  Assessment of growth and
  developmental milestones,
  particularly in children, to identify
  any concerns that may be associated
  with seizures or underlying
  conditions.

4.2 Neurological tests

Neurological tests are diagnostic procedures
used to evaluate the function of the nervous
system, including the brain, spinal cord, and
peripheral nerves. These tests can help diagnose
neurological conditions, such as epilepsy, and
monitor the progression of the disease. Here are
some common neurological tests used in the
evaluation of epilepsy:

1. **Electroencephalogram (EEG)**: An
   EEG is a test that measures
   electrical activity in the brain. It is
   used to detect abnormal patterns of
   brain waves, which can indicate the
   presence of epilepsy or other

neurological disorders. During an EEG, electrodes are placed on the scalp, and the electrical activity of the brain is recorded.

2. **Video EEG Monitoring**: Video EEG monitoring combines video recording with EEG to capture both the physical manifestations of seizures and the corresponding brain wave patterns. This test is often used to help diagnose epilepsy and determine the type of seizures a person is experiencing.

3. **MRI (Magnetic Resonance Imaging)**: An MRI uses magnetic fields and radio waves to create detailed images of the brain. It can help identify structural abnormalities, such as tumors, cysts, or scar tissue, that may be causing seizures or other neurological symptoms.

4. **CT (Computed Tomography) Scan**: A CT scan uses X-rays to

create cross-sectional images of the brain. It is often used to detect abnormalities, such as bleeding or tumors, that may be associated with seizures.

5. **Neuropsychological Testing**: Neuropsychological testing assesses cognitive function, such as memory, attention, language, and problem-solving skills. It can help identify cognitive deficits that may be associated with epilepsy or the effects of seizures on the brain.

6. **SPECT (Single-Photon Emission Computed Tomography)**: SPECT imaging uses a radioactive tracer to create 3D images of blood flow in the brain. It can help identify areas of the brain that are affected by seizures and may be useful in localizing the seizure focus.

7. **PET (Positron Emission Tomography) Scan**: A PET scan uses a radioactive tracer to measure

brain activity. It can help identify areas of the brain that are hyperactive or hypoactive, which may be associated with seizures or other neurological conditions.

8. **Functional MRI (fMRI)**: fMRI measures changes in blood flow in the brain that are associated with brain activity. It can help identify areas of the brain that are involved in specific functions, such as language or motor skills, and may be useful in planning epilepsy surgery.

4.3 Electroencephalogram (EEG)

An electroencephalogram (EEG) is a non-invasive test that records the electrical activity of the brain. It is used to detect abnormalities in the brain's electrical patterns, which can help diagnose various neurological conditions, including epilepsy. Here's a detailed explanation of how an EEG works and its uses in diagnosing and managing epilepsy:

How Does an EEG Work? During an EEG, electrodes are attached to the scalp using a sticky paste or cap. These electrodes detect the electrical signals produced by the brain's neurons. The signals are amplified and recorded as a series of wavy lines called brain waves. EEG patterns can vary depending on the state of the brain, such as during wakefulness, sleep, or during a seizure.

Types of EEG Recordings:

- **Routine EEG**: A standard EEG recording typically lasts 20-30 minutes and is done with the patient awake and relaxed. The test may also include specific tasks or stimuli to provoke certain brain responses.
- **Sleep EEG**: Sometimes, an EEG is performed while the patient is asleep to record brain activity during different

stages of sleep. This can help detect abnormalities that may be more prominent during sleep.

- **Ambulatory EEG**: In some cases, an EEG may be done over a longer period, such as 24 hours or more, to capture more data and increase the likelihood of recording a seizure if it occurs infrequently.

Uses of EEG in Epilepsy:

- **Diagnosis**: EEG is used to help diagnose epilepsy by detecting abnormal brain wave patterns characteristic of seizures. The test can also help determine the type of epilepsy based on the pattern of abnormalities.
- **Seizure Classification**: EEG can help classify seizures as focal or generalized based on the origin of abnormal electrical activity in the brain.
- **Treatment Planning**: EEG findings can help guide treatment decisions, such as the

choice of antiepileptic medications or the consideration of surgical options.

- **Monitoring**: EEG is used to monitor the effectiveness of treatment and to track changes in brain activity over time.

Interpreting EEG Results:

1. **Normal EEG**: A normal EEG shows a regular pattern of brain waves and no signs of abnormal activity.

2. **Abnormal EEG**: An abnormal EEG may show spikes, sharp waves, or other patterns indicative of epilepsy or other neurological disorders. The location and nature of these abnormalities can provide valuable information about the type and origin of seizures.

4.4 Imaging tests (MRI, CT scan)

Imaging tests, such as MRI (Magnetic Resonance Imaging) and CT (Computed Tomography) scans, are commonly used in the evaluation of epilepsy to visualize the structure of the brain and identify any abnormalities that may be causing seizures. Here's a detailed explanation of each imaging test:

MRI (Magnetic Resonance Imaging):

- **How it Works**: MRI uses a strong magnetic field and radio waves to create detailed images of the brain. It provides high-resolution images that can show the structure of the brain, including the presence of tumors, scar tissue, or other abnormalities.
- **Uses in Epilepsy**: MRI is used to identify structural abnormalities that may be associated with epilepsy, such as tumors, cortical dysplasia (abnormal brain

development), hippocampal sclerosis (damage to the hippocampus), or vascular malformations.

- **Procedure**: During an MRI, the patient lies on a table that slides into a large, tunnel-like machine. The procedure is painless but requires the patient to remain still, as movement can blur the images.
- **Types of MRI**: Different types of MRI sequences, such as T1-weighted, T2-weighted, and FLAIR (Fluid-Attenuated Inversion Recovery), may be used to visualize different aspects of brain structure and pathology.

CT (Computed Tomography) Scan:

- **How it Works**: CT uses X-rays to create cross-sectional images of the brain. It provides detailed images that can show the structure of the brain and detect abnormalities such as tumors, bleeding, or structural changes.
- **Uses in Epilepsy**: CT is often used as an initial imaging test in the emergency

setting to rule out acute conditions such as bleeding or stroke. It can also detect structural abnormalities that may be associated with epilepsy.

- **Procedure**: During a CT scan, the patient lies on a table that slides into a doughnut-shaped machine. The procedure is quick and painless, but it does involve exposure to X-ray radiation.
- **Contrast**: In some cases, a contrast dye may be injected into a vein to enhance the visibility of certain structures or abnormalities on the CT images.

Comparison:

- MRI is preferred over CT for evaluating epilepsy because it provides higher resolution images and does not involve exposure to ionizing radiation.
- CT is faster and more readily available than MRI, making it useful in emergency situations where quick imaging is needed.

Chapter 5

Treatment Options

5.1 Antiepileptic drugs (AEDs)

Antiepileptic drugs (AEDs), also known as antiseizure or anticonvulsant medications, are a class of medications used to treat epilepsy and prevent seizures. These drugs work by reducing the abnormal electrical activity in the brain that leads to seizures. Here's a detailed explanation of AEDs:

Mechanism of Action:

- AEDs act on various neurotransmitter systems in the brain, such as gamma-aminobutyric acid (GABA), glutamate, and voltage-gated ion channels, to stabilize neuronal membranes and inhibit the spread of abnormal electrical activity.

- Different AEDs target different mechanisms, which is why multiple medications are available to treat epilepsy, each with its own unique profile of efficacy and side effects.

Types of AEDs:

- There are many different AEDs available, and they are classified based on their mechanism of action:
  - **GABAergic Agents**: Enhance the inhibitory effects of GABA, reducing neuronal excitability. Examples include benzodiazepines (e.g., clonazepam), valproate, and vigabatrin.
  - **Sodium Channel Blockers**: Inhibit the influx of sodium ions, preventing the rapid firing of neurons. Examples include carbamazepine, phenytoin, and lamotrigine.
  - **Calcium Channel Blockers**: Inhibit the influx of calcium ions,

which can reduce neurotransmitter release. Examples include ethosuximide and gabapentin.
  - **Glutamate Receptor Antagonists**: Block the effects of the excitatory neurotransmitter glutamate. Examples include topiramate and felbamate.
- Some AEDs have multiple mechanisms of action, providing a broader spectrum of efficacy.

Indications:

- AEDs are primarily used to prevent seizures in individuals with epilepsy.
- They may also be used to treat other conditions, such as neuropathic pain, bipolar disorder, and migraine headaches, due to their effects on neuronal excitability.

Treatment Considerations:

- AED selection is based on the type of epilepsy, seizure frequency, age, sex, and other individual factors.
- Some AEDs are more effective for specific types of seizures (e.g., focal vs. generalized seizures), so a thorough evaluation is necessary.
- AEDs are typically started at a low dose and gradually increased to achieve optimal seizure control while minimizing side effects.
- Regular monitoring, including blood tests and EEGs, may be needed to assess the effectiveness and safety of AEDs.

Side Effects:

- Common side effects of AEDs include dizziness, drowsiness, fatigue, and gastrointestinal disturbances.
- Some AEDs may cause more serious side effects, such as liver toxicity, allergic reactions, or psychiatric symptoms. Monitoring is important to detect and manage these side effects.

Drug Interactions:

AEDs can interact with other medications, affecting their efficacy or increasing the risk of side effects. It is important to review all medications with a healthcare provider before starting an AED.

5.2 Surgery

Surgery is a treatment option for epilepsy that may be considered when medications are ineffective in controlling seizures. It involves removing or altering brain tissue that is causing the seizures. Here's a detailed explanation of epilepsy surgery:

Types of Epilepsy Surgery:

1. **Resective Surgery:** This type of surgery involves removing the part of the brain that is causing seizures. It is most commonly performed for focal epilepsy when seizures originate from a specific area of the brain that can be safely

removed without causing significant neurological deficits.

2. **Lesionectomy**: This procedure involves removing a brain lesion, such as a tumor or scar tissue, that is causing seizures.

3. **Lobectomy**: Lobectomy involves removing a lobe of the brain, such as the temporal lobe, where seizures are originating.

4. **Hemispherectomy**: In rare cases of severe epilepsy that affects an entire hemisphere of the brain, a hemispherectomy may be performed to disconnect or remove the affected hemisphere.

5. **Corpus Callosotomy**: This procedure involves cutting the corpus callosum, the bundle of nerves that connects the two hemispheres of the brain, to prevent seizures from spreading from one side of the brain to the other.

6. **Multiple Subpial Transection** (MST): MST is a procedure that involves making small cuts in the brain to disrupt the

spread of seizures while preserving
normal brain function.

Evaluation for Surgery:

- Before surgery, a comprehensive
  evaluation is conducted to determine if the
  patient is a candidate for surgery. This
  evaluation may include:
    - Video EEG monitoring to pinpoint
      the origin of seizures.
    - Neuropsychological testing to
      assess cognitive function.
    - MRI or other imaging tests to
      identify the location of the seizure
      focus.
    - Wada test to assess language and
      memory functions in the brain.

Surgical Procedure:

- Epilepsy surgery is typically performed
  under general anesthesia.
- The surgical team uses advanced imaging
  techniques and intraoperative monitoring

to precisely locate and remove or disconnect the seizure focus while minimizing damage to surrounding brain tissue.

Recovery and Outcomes:

- Recovery from epilepsy surgery varies depending on the type of surgery and individual factors. Most patients require a hospital stay after surgery and may experience some temporary side effects, such as headaches, fatigue, or memory difficulties.
- The success rate of epilepsy surgery varies depending on the type of surgery and the underlying cause of epilepsy. Overall, surgery can be highly effective in reducing or eliminating seizures in many patients.

Risks and Complications:

Epilepsy surgery is a major procedure that carries risks, including infection, bleeding, and neurological deficits. The risks and benefits of surgery are carefully weighed before a decision is made to proceed.

5.3 Vagus nerve stimulation (VNS)

Vagus nerve stimulation (VNS) is a treatment for epilepsy that involves implanting a device that delivers electrical impulses to the vagus nerve, which is a large nerve that runs from the brain through the neck and into the chest and abdomen. VNS is used to help prevent seizures by modulating the electrical activity in the brain. Here's a detailed explanation of VNS:

How VNS Works:

- The VNS device is implanted under the skin in the chest, and a wire is threaded under the skin to the vagus nerve in the neck.
- The device delivers regular, mild electrical impulses to the vagus nerve, which then sends these impulses to the brain.

- It is believed that these electrical impulses can help regulate abnormal brain activity that leads to seizures.

Indications for VNS:

- VNS is typically considered for individuals with epilepsy who have not responded well to medications.
- It may be used in both focal and generalized epilepsy.

Implantation Procedure:

- The VNS device is implanted during a surgical procedure that typically takes about an hour.
- The device is placed under the skin in the chest, and the wire is threaded under the skin to the vagus nerve in the neck.
- The device is programmed by a healthcare provider to deliver the appropriate amount of stimulation.

Adjusting the Device:

- The VNS device is programmed to deliver electrical impulses at regular intervals.
- The device can also be activated manually by holding a magnet over the device, which can help stop or shorten a seizure if one is occurring.

Effectiveness:

- VNS is not a cure for epilepsy, but it can help reduce the frequency and severity of seizures in some individuals.
- It may take several months for the full effects of VNS to be seen, and the device may need to be adjusted over time to optimize its effectiveness.

Side Effects:

- The most common side effects of VNS are hoarseness, throat pain, and coughing, which are typically mild and improve over time.

- Other side effects may include shortness of breath, difficulty swallowing, and tingling in the neck or throat.

Risks:

As with any surgical procedure, there are risks associated with implanting the VNS device, including infection, bleeding, and damage to surrounding structures.

There is also a risk of the device malfunctioning or not providing the desired level of seizure control.

5.4 Ketogenic diet

The ketogenic diet is a high-fat, low-carbohydrate diet that has been used since the 1920s as a treatment for epilepsy, particularly in children who have not responded well to medication. The diet is designed to mimic the metabolic effects of fasting, leading to the production of ketones, which are molecules produced by the liver from fatty acids.

Mechanism of Action:

- When carbohydrates are restricted, the body enters a state of ketosis, where it burns fat for fuel instead of carbohydrates.
- Ketones, which are produced during ketosis, are believed to have anticonvulsant properties that help reduce seizure activity in the brain.

Composition of the Ketogenic Diet:

- The ketogenic diet is high in fats, typically providing around 70-80% of total daily calories.
- Protein intake is moderate, accounting for around 15-20% of total calories.
- Carbohydrate intake is very low, usually less than 50 grams per day, or around 5-10% of total calories.

Types of Ketogenic Diets:

1. **Classic Ketogenic Diet**: This is the most restrictive form of the diet, with a ratio of fat to combined protein and carbohydrates

of 4:1 or 3:1. This means that for every gram of protein and carbohydrate, there are 4 or 3 grams of fat, respectively.

2. **Modified Atkins Diet**: This diet is less restrictive than the classic ketogenic diet and allows for more protein and carbohydrates. The fat to protein and carbohydrate ratio is around 1:1 or 2:1.

3. **MCT (Medium-Chain Triglyceride) Ketogenic Diet**: This diet includes more medium-chain triglycerides, which are more easily converted into ketones by the liver. This allows for a slightly higher carbohydrate intake compared to the classic ketogenic diet.

Indications for the Ketogenic Diet:

- The ketogenic diet is primarily used as a treatment for epilepsy, particularly in children with refractory epilepsy who have not responded well to medication.
- It may also be used as a treatment for certain metabolic disorders, such as glucose transporter type 1 deficiency

syndrome (GLUT1 DS) and pyruvate
dehydrogenase deficiency.

Effectiveness:

- The ketogenic diet has been shown to be effective in reducing seizures in children with refractory epilepsy. Studies have reported seizure reduction of 50% or more in about half of the children who try the diet.
- The diet may be particularly effective for certain types of epilepsy, such as Dravet syndrome and Lennox-Gastaut syndrome.

Adverse Effects:

The ketogenic diet can cause side effects, particularly in the initial stages when the body is adapting to ketosis. These side effects may include constipation, vomiting, diarrhea, and low blood sugar.

Long-term side effects may include kidney stones, low bone mineral density, and growth retardation in children.

5.5 Lifestyle and self-management

Lifestyle and self-management strategies play an important role in the management of epilepsy. These strategies can help improve overall health, reduce seizure frequency and severity, and enhance quality of life. Here are some key components of lifestyle and self-management for epilepsy:

1. **Medication Adherence**:

   - It's crucial to take antiepileptic medications exactly as prescribed by a healthcare provider. Missing doses or stopping medication abruptly can increase the risk of seizures.

2. **Stress Management**:

   - Stress can trigger seizures in some individuals. Practicing stress-reducing techniques such as deep breathing, meditation, yoga, or regular physical activity can help manage stress levels.

3. **Sleep**:

- Getting enough sleep is important for overall health and can help reduce the risk of seizures. Establishing a regular sleep schedule, creating a relaxing bedtime routine, and avoiding caffeine and electronics before bed can promote better sleep.

4. **Nutrition:**

- A balanced diet can support overall health and may help reduce seizure frequency in some individuals. Some people with epilepsy find that following a ketogenic diet, which is high in fats and low in carbohydrates, can help control seizures.

5. **Avoiding Triggers:**

- Identifying and avoiding triggers that may increase the risk of seizures can be helpful. Common triggers include lack of sleep, stress, alcohol, and certain foods or food additives.

6. Safety Precautions:

- Taking safety precautions, such as wearing a helmet for activities that carry a risk of head injury and avoiding activities that could be dangerous during a seizure, can help prevent injuries.

7. Regular Exercise:

- Regular physical activity can help improve overall health and may help reduce stress and improve mood. It's important to choose activities that are safe and appropriate for your condition.

8. Monitoring and Journaling:

- Keeping a seizure diary or journal can help track seizure activity, identify triggers, and monitor the effectiveness of treatment. This information can be valuable for healthcare providers in managing your condition.

9. Education and Support:

- Educating yourself about epilepsy and staying informed about treatment options and lifestyle strategies can empower you to manage your condition effectively. Support groups and counseling can also provide valuable support and guidance.

10. Healthcare Provider Communication:

- Maintaining open communication with your healthcare provider is essential. Regular check-ups and discussions about your treatment plan can help ensure that your epilepsy is well-managed.

Chapter 6

Managing Epilepsy in Adults

6.1 Medication adherence

Medication adherence, also known as medication compliance, refers to the extent to which individuals follow the prescribed medication regimen as instructed by their healthcare provider. For people with epilepsy, adherence to antiepileptic medications is crucial for controlling seizures and maintaining overall health. Here's a detailed explanation of medication adherence:

> **Understanding the Importance**: Adherence to antiepileptic medications is essential for seizure control. Consistently taking medications as prescribed can significantly reduce the frequency and severity of seizures, allowing individuals to lead more active and fulfilling lives.

Following the Prescribed Schedule: Healthcare providers typically prescribe specific doses of antiepileptic medications to be taken at certain times of the day. It's important for individuals to follow this schedule closely, taking the medications at the same time each day to maintain steady levels in the bloodstream.

Avoiding Missed Doses: Missing doses of antiepileptic medications can increase the risk of breakthrough seizures. Individuals should make every effort to take their medications as scheduled. Setting reminders, using pill organizers, or incorporating medication-taking into daily routines can help reduce the likelihood of missed doses.

Communicating with Healthcare Providers: If individuals experience challenges or concerns related to their medication regimen, it's important for them to communicate openly with their healthcare provider. This includes discussing any side effects, difficulties with adherence, or changes in seizure frequency. Healthcare providers can offer support, adjust medications if necessary, or provide strategies to improve adherence.

Refilling Prescriptions on Time: Running out of medication can disrupt the treatment regimen and increase the risk of seizures. Individuals should ensure they have an adequate supply of medication and refill prescriptions in a timely manner, especially when traveling or during holidays when pharmacies may have limited hours.

Understanding the Importance of Long-Term Treatment: Epilepsy is typically a chronic condition that requires ongoing treatment. Even if seizures are well-controlled, it's important for individuals to continue taking their medications as prescribed to maintain seizure control and prevent recurrence.

Managing Side Effects: Some antiepileptic medications may cause side effects such as drowsiness, dizziness, or gastrointestinal discomfort. It's important for individuals to discuss any side effects with their healthcare provider rather than discontinuing the medication abruptly. Healthcare providers can often adjust the dosage or recommend strategies to minimize side effects while maintaining seizure control.

Incorporating Medication Adherence into Daily Routine: Establishing a regular routine for taking medications can help improve adherence. Individuals can incorporate medication-taking into daily activities such as meals or bedtime to make it a habit.

Seeking Support: Family members, caregivers, or support groups can provide encouragement and assistance with medication adherence. Having a supportive network can help individuals stay motivated and accountable for their treatment regimen.

Monitoring Progress: Regular follow-up appointments with healthcare providers are important for monitoring seizure control, adjusting medications as needed, and addressing any concerns related to adherence or treatment efficacy.

6.2 Driving and employment considerations

Certainly! Driving and employment considerations are important aspects of living with epilepsy, as they can impact an individual's independence, safety, and financial stability. Here's a detailed explanation of each:

Driving Considerations:

1. **Legal Requirements**: Laws regarding driving with epilepsy vary by country and jurisdiction. In many places, individuals with epilepsy are required to meet specific

criteria regarding seizure control and medication adherence in order to obtain or maintain a driver's license.

2. **Seizure-Free Period**: In most regions, individuals with epilepsy must typically remain seizure-free for a certain period of time before they are allowed to drive. This seizure-free period, often referred to as a "license suspension period," varies depending on local regulations and may range from several months to several years.

3. **Medical Review**: Some jurisdictions require individuals with epilepsy to undergo periodic medical reviews to assess their seizure control and overall fitness to drive. These reviews may involve evaluations by neurologists or other healthcare professionals specializing in epilepsy management.

4. **Reporting Seizures**: Individuals with epilepsy are often required to report any seizures to the relevant authorities, such as the Department of Motor Vehicles (DMV)

or licensing agency. Failure to report seizures can result in legal consequences and may jeopardize driving privileges.

5. **Driving Restrictions**: In some cases, individuals with epilepsy may be subject to certain driving restrictions or conditions, such as driving only during daylight hours, avoiding high-speed highways, or using vehicles equipped with automatic transmission and additional safety features.

6. **Safety Precautions**: It's important for individuals with epilepsy to prioritize safety when driving. This includes taking prescribed medications as directed, avoiding potential seizure triggers such as sleep deprivation or alcohol consumption, and following any additional recommendations provided by healthcare providers.

Employment Considerations:

1. **Legal Protections**: Individuals with epilepsy are protected from discrimination

in the workplace under laws such as the Americans with Disabilities Act (ADA) in the United States and similar legislation in other countries. Employers are generally prohibited from discriminating against individuals with epilepsy based on their medical condition.

2. **Disclosure**: While individuals with epilepsy are not required to disclose their medical condition to employers, they may choose to do so in order to request reasonable accommodations or to ensure that appropriate safety measures are in place.

3. **Reasonable Accommodations**: Employers are required to provide reasonable accommodations to individuals with epilepsy, such as flexible work schedules, modifications to job duties or work environments, or time off for medical appointments.

4. **Safety Considerations**: In certain industries or positions, safety concerns related to epilepsy may arise. Employers

have a responsibility to assess potential risks and implement appropriate safety measures to protect both employees with epilepsy and their coworkers.

5. **Workplace Support**: Creating a supportive work environment can contribute to the success and well-being of employees with epilepsy. This may involve providing education and training on epilepsy awareness, fostering open communication, and offering resources for managing the condition effectively.

6. **Career Planning**: Individuals with epilepsy may benefit from career counseling or guidance to explore career options that align with their abilities, interests, and medical needs. Seeking opportunities for professional development and advancement can help individuals with epilepsy achieve their career goals.

By understanding and addressing the driving and employment considerations associated with epilepsy, individuals can take steps to navigate these aspects of daily life effectively while managing their condition and pursuing their personal and professional goals.

6.3 Pregnancy and contraception

Certainly! Pregnancy and contraception are important considerations for women with epilepsy due to the potential impact of seizures and antiepileptic medications on pregnancy and fetal development. Here's a detailed explanation of each:

Pregnancy Considerations:

1. **Planning Pregnancy**: Women with epilepsy who are planning to become pregnant should discuss their plans with their healthcare provider. Preconception counseling can help ensure that the pregnancy is as safe and healthy as possible.

2. **Medication Management**: It's important for women with epilepsy to continue taking their antiepileptic medications during pregnancy, as uncontrolled seizures can pose risks to both the mother and the fetus. However, some antiepileptic medications may increase the risk of birth defects or other complications.

3. **Seizure Control**: Maintaining good seizure control is crucial during pregnancy. Healthcare providers may need to adjust medication dosages or prescribe different medications to achieve optimal seizure control while minimizing risks to the fetus.

4. **Prenatal Care**: Women with epilepsy should receive regular prenatal care throughout pregnancy. This may involve more frequent monitoring and testing to assess the health of both the mother and the fetus.

5. **Risks and Complications**: Pregnancy in women with epilepsy is considered high-risk due to the potential for seizures,

medication-related complications, and other factors. Close monitoring by healthcare providers can help mitigate these risks.

6. **Delivery Planning**: Women with epilepsy should discuss their delivery plans with their healthcare provider. In some cases, a cesarean section may be recommended to reduce the risk of injury during delivery if seizures are not well-controlled.

7. **Postpartum Care**: After delivery, women with epilepsy should continue to receive medical care and monitoring. Changes in medication dosages or types may be necessary, as hormonal changes after pregnancy can affect seizure control.

Contraception Considerations:

1. **Birth Control Options**: Women with epilepsy have several contraceptive options available to them. However, some antiepileptic medications can interact with hormonal contraceptives, potentially reducing their effectiveness.

2. **Hormonal Contraceptives**: Some antiepileptic medications can reduce the effectiveness of hormonal contraceptives, such as birth control pills, patches, and rings. Women taking these medications may need to use additional forms of contraception or consider non-hormonal options.

3. **Non-Hormonal Contraceptives**: Non-hormonal contraceptive options, such as barrier methods (e.g., condoms, diaphragms) or intrauterine devices (IUDs), may be more suitable for women with epilepsy taking certain antiepileptic medications.

4. **Family Planning**: Women with epilepsy who are considering pregnancy should discuss their plans with their healthcare provider. Preconception counseling can help ensure that they are taking appropriate precautions and managing their medication regimen safely.

5. **Medication Adjustments**: Women with epilepsy who are taking hormonal

contraceptives should be aware that changes in medication dosages or types may be necessary if they become pregnant or if they experience changes in their seizure control.

By carefully managing pregnancy and contraception, women with epilepsy can help ensure the best possible outcomes for themselves and their babies while effectively managing their condition. Consulting with healthcare providers who have expertise in epilepsy and pregnancy is essential for personalized guidance and care.

Chapter 7

Managing Epilepsy in Children

7.1 Special considerations for pediatric patients

Special considerations for pediatric patients with epilepsy include unique challenges related to diagnosis, treatment, and management. Here's a detailed explanation:

1. **Diagnosis and Evaluation**: Diagnosing epilepsy in children can be challenging due to the wide range of seizure types and presentations. Pediatric neurologists often rely on a combination of medical history, physical examination, EEG (electroencephalogram), and imaging studies to make an accurate diagnosis.

2. **Seizure Types**: Children may experience different types of seizures compared to adults. Some seizures may be subtle and difficult to recognize, such as absence

seizures, which can affect a child's attention and awareness without causing convulsions.

3. **Impact on Development**: Epilepsy can impact a child's development, including cognition, behavior, and social skills. Early detection and appropriate management are important to minimize the impact of epilepsy on a child's development and quality of life.

4. **Treatment Approach**: The goal of treatment in pediatric epilepsy is to achieve seizure control with minimal side effects. Medication selection is based on the type of epilepsy, seizure frequency, age of the child, and potential side effects. Dosages are often adjusted based on the child's weight and age.

5. **Medication Adherence**: Ensuring medication adherence can be challenging in pediatric patients. Parents and caregivers play a crucial role in helping children take their medications as prescribed. Healthcare providers may

provide tools and strategies to improve adherence, such as pill organizers or reminder systems.

6. **Education and Support**: Providing education and support to parents, caregivers, and children is important. This includes information about epilepsy, its management, safety precautions, and how to recognize and respond to seizures.

7. **Psychosocial Support**: Children with epilepsy may face social and emotional challenges. Psychosocial support, such as counseling and support groups, can help children and their families cope with the challenges of living with epilepsy.

8. **Education and School Accommodations**: Children with epilepsy may require special accommodations at school, such as a seizure action plan, trained staff to respond to seizures, and adjustments to their learning environment to ensure their safety and well-being.

9. **Transition to Adulthood**: As children with epilepsy transition to adulthood, they

may need additional support and guidance to manage their condition independently. Transition programs can help prepare adolescents for managing their epilepsy as adults.

10.   **Monitoring and Follow-up**: Regular monitoring and follow-up with a pediatric neurologist are essential to assess seizure control, medication effectiveness, and any potential side effects. Adjustments to the treatment plan may be necessary over time.

Managing epilepsy in pediatric patients requires a comprehensive and multidisciplinary approach that addresses the unique needs and challenges faced by children and their families. Collaboration between healthcare providers, parents, caregivers, and educators is key to ensuring the best possible outcomes for children with epilepsy.

7.2 School accommodations

School accommodations for children with epilepsy are crucial to ensure their safety, well-being, and academic success. Here's a detailed explanation of the types of accommodations that may be necessary:

Seizure Action Plan: A seizure action plan outlines specific steps to be taken in the event of a seizure. It includes information on the child's seizure type, triggers, medications, and emergency contacts. School staff should be trained on how to recognize and respond to seizures according to the plan.

Medication Management: Some children with epilepsy may require medication during school hours. Schools should have a policy and procedures in place for administering medication safely, including storage and documentation. Parents or caregivers may need to provide written consent and instructions for medication administration.

Educational Support: Children with epilepsy may benefit from educational support, such as additional time for assignments and tests, modified homework or classroom activities, or access to tutoring services. Individualized Education Programs (IEPs) or 504 Plans can outline these accommodations and ensure they are implemented.

Safety Precautions: Schools should take steps to create a safe environment for children with epilepsy. This may include removing hazards that could cause injury during a seizure, ensuring that staff are trained in seizure first aid, and providing supervision during activities that may pose a higher risk for seizures.

Emotional Support: Living with epilepsy can be challenging, and children may benefit from emotional support. Schools can provide access to counseling services or support groups to help children cope with the emotional aspects of their condition.

Communication Plan: Schools should have a communication plan in place to ensure that parents, caregivers, and school staff are informed about the child's epilepsy and any changes to their condition or treatment plan. This can help ensure a coordinated and supportive approach to managing the child's epilepsy at school.

Awareness and Education: Educating school staff, students, and parents about epilepsy can help reduce stigma and increase understanding. Schools can provide information about epilepsy, its impact, and how to support children with the condition.

Emergency Preparedness: Schools should have protocols in place for managing seizures and other medical emergencies. This may include having staff trained in CPR and first aid, as well as ensuring access to emergency medical services if needed.

Physical Education and Sports: Children with epilepsy can participate in physical activities and sports, but certain precautions may be necessary. Schools should work with healthcare providers to determine appropriate levels of activity and any necessary accommodations.

Transition Planning: As children with epilepsy transition to new schools or grade levels, it's important to ensure that accommodations are in place and that new school staff are informed about the child's needs. Transition planning can help ensure a smooth transition and continuity of care.

7.3 Developmental impact

The developmental impact of epilepsy on children can vary depending on factors such as the age of onset, seizure frequency and severity, type of epilepsy, and the effectiveness of treatment. Here's a detailed explanation of how epilepsy can impact development:

1. **Cognitive Development**: Epilepsy can affect cognitive development, including attention, memory, language skills, and executive function. Seizures and the underlying brain abnormalities associated with epilepsy can disrupt normal brain development, leading to cognitive challenges.

2. **Behavioral Development**: Children with epilepsy may experience behavioral issues, such as hyperactivity, impulsivity, and emotional difficulties. These behavioral problems can be a result of the underlying brain abnormalities, the impact

of seizures, or the side effects of antiepileptic medications.

3. **Academic Achievement**: Epilepsy can impact academic achievement due to cognitive and behavioral challenges. Children with epilepsy may have difficulty with learning, memory, and attention, which can affect their performance in school.

4. **Social Development**: Social development can be affected by epilepsy, as children may experience stigma, social isolation, and difficulties forming and maintaining relationships. Social challenges can arise due to the unpredictable nature of seizures and the misconceptions surrounding epilepsy.

5. **Emotional Development**: Epilepsy can impact emotional development, leading to increased anxiety, depression, and low self-esteem. Children with epilepsy may struggle with the emotional consequences of living with a chronic medical condition,

as well as the social challenges that can accompany it.

6. **Quality of Life**: The impact of epilepsy on development can significantly affect the quality of life of children and their families. Managing epilepsy requires ongoing medical care, which can be stressful and time-consuming. The social and emotional challenges associated with epilepsy can also impact quality of life.

7. **Educational Support**: Providing educational support, such as individualized education plans (IEPs) or 504 plans, can help address the academic challenges faced by children with epilepsy. These plans can include accommodations such as extra time for tests, modified assignments, and access to support services.

8. **Psychosocial Support**: Psychosocial support, including counseling and support groups, can help children and families cope with the emotional and social challenges of living with epilepsy. It can

also provide strategies for managing stress and improving quality of life.

9. **Early Intervention**: Early intervention services can be beneficial for children with epilepsy to address developmental delays and provide support for optimal development. These services may include speech therapy, occupational therapy, and behavioral therapy.

10. **Monitoring and Management**: Regular monitoring and management of epilepsy are essential to minimize the impact on development. This includes working closely with healthcare providers to ensure that seizures are well-controlled and that any cognitive or behavioral issues are addressed promptly.

Chapter 8

Living with Epilepsy

8.1 Psychological and social challenges

Living with epilepsy can present various psychological and social challenges for individuals. Here's a detailed explanation of these challenges:

Psychological Challenges:

1. **Stigma and Misconceptions:** There is still a stigma attached to epilepsy in many societies, leading to misconceptions and discrimination against individuals with the condition. This stigma can impact self-esteem, mental health, and social interactions.

2. **Anxiety and Depression**: The unpredictability of seizures and the impact of epilepsy on daily life can lead to

feelings of anxiety and depression. These mental health issues can be exacerbated by concerns about safety, social acceptance, and the future.

3. **Coping with Uncertainty**: Epilepsy is often unpredictable, with seizures occurring without warning. This uncertainty can lead to feelings of fear, stress, and a sense of loss of control over one's life.

4. **Fear of Seizures**: The fear of having a seizure in public or in certain situations can be overwhelming for individuals with epilepsy. This fear can lead to social isolation and avoidance of activities that may trigger anxiety.

5. **Cognitive Challenges**: Some individuals with epilepsy may experience cognitive challenges, such as memory problems, difficulty concentrating, and slowed thinking. These challenges can impact academic and occupational performance, as well as daily functioning.

6. **Impact on Self-Image:** Epilepsy can affect how individuals see themselves, leading to changes in self-image and identity. Adjusting to life with epilepsy may require reevaluating one's goals, aspirations, and sense of self.

Social Challenges:

1. **Social Isolation**: Due to fear of seizures or stigma associated with epilepsy, individuals may withdraw from social activities and isolate themselves from friends and family. This can lead to feelings of loneliness and depression.

2. **Relationships**: Epilepsy can impact relationships with family, friends, and romantic partners. Misunderstandings about the condition and concerns about safety during seizures can strain relationships and lead to feelings of isolation.

3. **Educational and Occupational Challenges:** Epilepsy can impact educational and occupational

opportunities. Discrimination and lack of understanding about epilepsy in educational and workplace settings can create barriers to success.

4. **Safety Concerns:** Safety is a significant concern for individuals with epilepsy, especially during activities that may pose a risk of injury during a seizure. This can limit participation in certain activities and lead to feelings of restriction and frustration.

5. **Access to Care**: Access to quality healthcare, including epilepsy specialists and mental health services, can be challenging for some individuals. Limited access to care can impact the management of epilepsy and exacerbate psychological and social challenges.

6. **Financial Burden:** Managing epilepsy can be costly, with expenses related to medications, doctor visits, and treatments. Financial strain can add to the stress and anxiety experienced by individuals with epilepsy.

8.2 Support groups and resources

Support groups and resources play a crucial role in providing assistance, information, and emotional support to individuals living with epilepsy and their families. Here's a detailed explanation of support groups and resources:

Support Groups:

1. **Peer Support**: Support groups provide an opportunity for individuals with epilepsy to connect with others facing similar challenges. Peer support can reduce feelings of isolation and provide a sense of community and understanding.
2. **Information and Education**: Support groups often provide valuable information about epilepsy, its management, treatment options, and resources. This information can help individuals make informed decisions about their care.

3. **Emotional Support**: Living with epilepsy can be challenging, and support groups offer a safe space for individuals to express their feelings, share experiences, and receive empathy and encouragement from others.

4. **Practical Tips and Coping Strategies**: Support groups can provide practical tips and coping strategies for managing epilepsy, such as seizure first aid, stress management techniques, and strategies for improving quality of life.

5. **Advocacy and Awareness**: Some support groups engage in advocacy efforts to raise awareness about epilepsy, reduce stigma, and improve access to care and resources for individuals with epilepsy.

Resources:

1. **Epilepsy Foundation**: The Epilepsy Foundation is a leading resource for information, support, and advocacy for individuals with epilepsy and their families. The foundation offers

educational materials, support groups, and programs to improve the lives of those affected by epilepsy.

2. **National Institute of Neurological Disorders and Stroke (NINDS)**: NINDS provides information about epilepsy, research initiatives, and resources for individuals with epilepsy and their families. They also fund research to advance the understanding and treatment of epilepsy.

3. **Centers for Disease Control and Prevention (CDC)**: The CDC offers information about epilepsy, including data and statistics, educational materials, and resources for healthcare providers and public health professionals.

4. **Local Hospitals and Clinics**: Many hospitals and clinics offer resources and support services for individuals with epilepsy, including educational programs, support groups, and access to epilepsy specialists.

5. **Online Resources**: There are many online resources for individuals with epilepsy, including websites, forums, and social media groups where people can connect with others, share experiences, and access information and support.

6. **Government Agencies**: Government agencies, such as the Health Resources and Services Administration (HRSA) and the Substance Abuse and Mental Health Services Administration (SAMHSA), offer resources and programs to support individuals with epilepsy and their families.

7. **Nonprofit Organizations**: Nonprofit organizations dedicated to epilepsy, such as the Danny Did Foundation, offer resources, support, and advocacy for individuals with epilepsy and their families.

Chapter 9

Emerging Therapies and Research

9.1 Investigational treatments

Investigational treatments for epilepsy refer to therapies that are currently being studied in clinical trials or research settings. These treatments aim to improve seizure control, reduce side effects, and enhance the quality of life for individuals with epilepsy. Here's a detailed explanation of some investigational treatments:

1. **Responsive Neurostimulation (RNS):** RNS is a treatment that involves the implantation of a device in the brain that detects and responds to abnormal electrical activity associated with seizures. The device delivers small electrical pulses to disrupt seizure activity before it spreads in the brain.

2. **Deep Brain Stimulation (DBS)**: DBS is a treatment that involves the implantation of electrodes in specific areas of the brain. The electrodes deliver electrical stimulation to modulate brain activity and reduce seizure frequency.

3. **Vagus Nerve Stimulation (VNS)**: VNS is a treatment that involves the implantation of a device that stimulates the vagus nerve in the neck. VNS has been shown to reduce seizure frequency in some individuals with epilepsy.

4. **Transcranial Magnetic Stimulation (TMS)**: TMS is a non-invasive treatment that uses magnetic fields to stimulate nerve cells in the brain. TMS is being studied as a potential treatment for epilepsy, particularly for individuals who do not respond to medication.

5. **Cannabidiol (CBD)**: CBD is a compound derived from the cannabis plant that has shown promise in reducing seizure frequency in some forms of epilepsy, such as Dravet syndrome and Lennox-Gastaut

syndrome. Research is ongoing to better understand its effectiveness and safety.

6. **Gene Therapy**: Gene therapy involves modifying genes to treat or prevent disease. In epilepsy, gene therapy is being studied as a potential treatment to modify brain activity and reduce seizure frequency.

7. **Stem Cell Therapy**: Stem cell therapy involves using stem cells to replace damaged or malfunctioning cells in the brain. This therapy is being investigated as a potential treatment for epilepsy to repair the brain's neural circuits and reduce seizures.

8. **Dietary Therapies**: Various dietary therapies, such as the modified Atkins diet and the low glycemic index treatment (LGIT), are being studied for their effectiveness in reducing seizure frequency in individuals with epilepsy, particularly those who do not respond to medication.

9. **Neuroprotective Agents**:
   Neuroprotective agents are substances that protect the brain from damage and promote healing. These agents are being studied as potential treatments for epilepsy to prevent or reduce the severity of seizures.

It's important to note that investigational treatments are still being studied and may not be widely available or approved for use outside of clinical trials. Individuals with epilepsy who are interested in participating in a clinical trial should speak with their healthcare provider to determine if they are eligible and to discuss the potential risks and benefits of participating.

9.2 Current research trends

Current research trends in epilepsy focus on several key areas aimed at improving the understanding, diagnosis, treatment, and management of the condition. Here's a detailed explanation of some of the current research trends:

1. **Precision Medicine**: Precision medicine aims to tailor treatments to individual patients based on their unique genetic, biological, and environmental factors. Researchers are studying how genetic testing and biomarkers can help personalize treatment approaches for individuals with epilepsy, leading to more effective and targeted therapies.

2. **Advanced Imaging Techniques**: Advanced imaging techniques, such as functional magnetic resonance imaging (fMRI) and magnetoencephalography (MEG), are being used to better understand the underlying mechanisms of epilepsy and identify biomarkers for diagnosis and treatment monitoring.

3. **Neurostimulation Therapies**: Neurostimulation therapies, such as responsive neurostimulation (RNS),

deep brain stimulation (DBS), and transcranial magnetic stimulation (TMS), are being studied to determine their effectiveness in reducing seizure frequency and improving quality of life for individuals with epilepsy.

4. **Cannabidiol (CBD) Research**: CBD, a compound derived from the cannabis plant, has shown promise in reducing seizure frequency in certain forms of epilepsy, such as Dravet syndrome and Lennox-Gastaut syndrome. Researchers are continuing to study the safety and effectiveness of CBD as a treatment for epilepsy.

5. **Gene Therapy**: Gene therapy involves modifying genes to treat or prevent disease. Researchers are studying gene therapy approaches for epilepsy to modify brain activity and reduce seizure frequency,

particularly in individuals who do not respond to other treatments.

    a. **Dietary Therapies**: Various dietary therapies, such as the ketogenic diet and the modified Atkins diet, are being studied for their effectiveness in reducing seizure frequency and improving seizure control in individuals with epilepsy, including those with drug-resistant epilepsy.

7. **Biomarker Development**: Researchers are working to identify biomarkers, such as specific proteins or genetic markers, that can help predict seizure onset, monitor disease progression, and assess treatment response in individuals with epilepsy.

8. **Comorbidities and Quality of Life**: Studies are focusing on understanding and addressing the comorbidities associated with epilepsy, such as depression, anxiety,

and cognitive impairment, to improve the overall quality of life for individuals living with the condition.

9. **Epilepsy Surgery**: Advances in surgical techniques, such as laser interstitial thermal therapy (LITT) and minimally invasive surgery, are improving outcomes for individuals with epilepsy who are candidates for surgery to control seizures.

10. **Telemedicine and Remote Monitoring**: Telemedicine and remote monitoring technologies are being used to improve access to care for individuals with epilepsy, particularly in underserved areas, and to facilitate remote monitoring of seizure activity and treatment response.

Chapter 10

Conclusion

10.1 Summary of key points

Here is a summary of the key points discussed about epilepsy:

1. **Definition and Overview**: Epilepsy is a neurological disorder characterized by recurrent seizures, which are sudden, uncontrolled electrical disturbances in the brain.

2. **Causes**: Epilepsy can be caused by various factors, including genetic predisposition, brain injury, infection, or developmental disorders.

3. **Types of Seizures**: Seizures can be classified into two main categories: focal seizures, which originate in one area of the brain, and generalized seizures, which involve both sides of the brain.

4. **Diagnosis**: Diagnosis of epilepsy involves a thorough medical history, physical examination, neurological tests, and sometimes imaging studies such as EEG and MRI.

5. **Treatment**: Treatment for epilepsy typically involves antiepileptic medications to control seizures. In some cases, surgery, dietary therapies, or neurostimulation techniques may be recommended.

6. **Lifestyle and Self-Management**: Lifestyle modifications, such as maintaining a regular sleep schedule, managing stress, and avoiding seizure triggers, can help manage epilepsy.

7. **Driving and Employment Considerations**: Individuals with epilepsy may face restrictions on driving and may require accommodations in the workplace.

8. **Pregnancy and Contraception**: Women with epilepsy need to carefully manage their medication and treatment during

pregnancy to ensure the safety of both the mother and the baby.

9. **Special Considerations for Pediatric Patients:** Children with epilepsy may face unique challenges related to diagnosis, treatment, and development.

10. **Psychological and Social Challenges**: Epilepsy can impact mental health and social interactions, leading to feelings of stigma, anxiety, and depression.

11. **Support Groups and Resources:** Support groups and resources are available to provide information, education, and emotional support to individuals with epilepsy and their families.

12. **Investigational Treatments:** Current research in epilepsy focuses on precision medicine, advanced imaging techniques, neurostimulation therapies, gene therapy, and other innovative approaches to improve treatment outcomes.

By understanding these key points, individuals living with epilepsy and their families can better navigate the challenges of managing the condition and access the support and resources available to them.

10.2 Future outlook for epilepsy management.

The future outlook for epilepsy management is promising, with ongoing research and advancements aimed at improving seizure control, reducing side effects, and enhancing the quality of life for individuals living with epilepsy. Here's a detailed explanation of the future outlook for epilepsy management:

1. **Precision Medicine**: Precision medicine approaches, which tailor treatment to individual patients based on their unique genetic, biological, and environmental factors, are expected to play a larger role in epilepsy management. Genetic testing and biomarkers may help personalize

treatment approaches, leading to more effective and targeted therapies.

2. **Advanced Imaging Techniques**: Advanced imaging techniques, such as functional magnetic resonance imaging (fMRI) and magnetoencephalography (MEG), are providing deeper insights into the underlying mechanisms of epilepsy. These techniques may help identify biomarkers for diagnosis, treatment monitoring, and predicting treatment response.

3. **Neurostimulation Therapies**: Neurostimulation therapies, such as responsive neurostimulation (RNS), deep brain stimulation (DBS), and transcranial magnetic stimulation (TMS), are continuously being refined and studied. These therapies have shown promise in reducing seizure frequency and improving quality of life for individuals with epilepsy.

4. **Gene Therapy and Gene Editing**: Gene therapy approaches for epilepsy are being

studied to modify genes and alter brain activity to reduce seizure frequency. Gene editing technologies, such as CRISPR-Cas9, hold potential for correcting genetic mutations associated with epilepsy.

5. **Dietary Therapies**: Dietary therapies, such as the ketogenic diet and modified Atkins diet, continue to be studied for their effectiveness in reducing seizure frequency and improving seizure control, particularly in individuals with drug-resistant epilepsy.

6. **Cannabidiol (CBD) Research**: Research on CBD, a compound derived from the cannabis plant, is ongoing to better understand its safety and effectiveness in reducing seizure frequency in various forms of epilepsy. CBD has shown promise as a treatment for certain types of epilepsy, such as Dravet syndrome and Lennox-Gastaut syndrome.

7. **Comorbidities and Quality of Life**: Future research will likely focus on

addressing the comorbidities associated with epilepsy, such as depression, anxiety, and cognitive impairment, to improve the overall quality of life for individuals living with the condition.

8. **Telemedicine and Remote Monitoring**: Telemedicine and remote monitoring technologies are expected to play a larger role in epilepsy management, providing improved access to care, monitoring of seizure activity, and support for individuals with epilepsy, particularly in underserved areas.

9. **Patient-Centered Care**: There is a growing emphasis on patient-centered care in epilepsy management, with a focus on involving patients in treatment decisions, addressing their unique needs and preferences, and improving communication and coordination of care.

10. **Clinical Trials and Research Collaborations**: Continued investment in clinical trials and research collaborations is essential for advancing our

understanding of epilepsy and developing new and innovative treatments. Collaborations between researchers, healthcare providers, industry, and patient advocacy groups will be key to driving progress in epilepsy management.

Overall, the future outlook for epilepsy management is optimistic, with ongoing research and advancements expected to lead to more personalized, effective, and patient-centered approaches to managing the condition.